CARING FOR YOUR PET LOBSTER

...a complete guide

by Weston Arey

ISBN 0-89272-293-2

Typeset at New England Graphics, Gardiner, Me.
Printed at Capital City Press, Montpelier, Vt.

5 4 3 2 1

DOWN EAST BOOKS / Camden, Maine 04843

CONTENTS

KEEPING A LOBSTER AS A PET

It may sound like a crazy idea, but you'll see that with a little training, you too can begin to enjoy the fine rewards of having your own crustacean friend to share all your good times together.

BENEFITS OF A LOBSTER IN THE HOME

WAKEUP CALL

Lobsters all have a great sense of time. And they'll be sure you're out of bed in time for your morning walk. You don't even need to set the alarm!

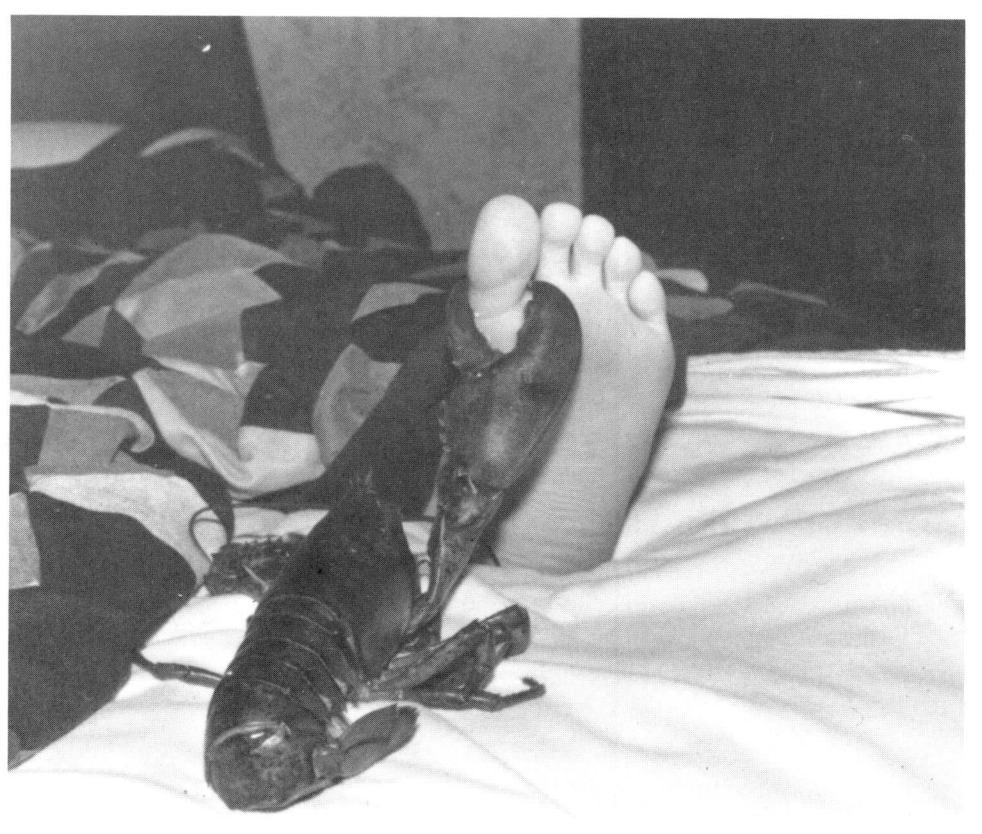

HOME SECURITY

Lobsters are all fiercely territorial. Pity the unwary burglar who tries to break in while your lobster's "on crawl!"

A HANDY NUTCRACKER

Your lobster may not want to eat nuts himself but he will be happy to help you get into your favorite snack.

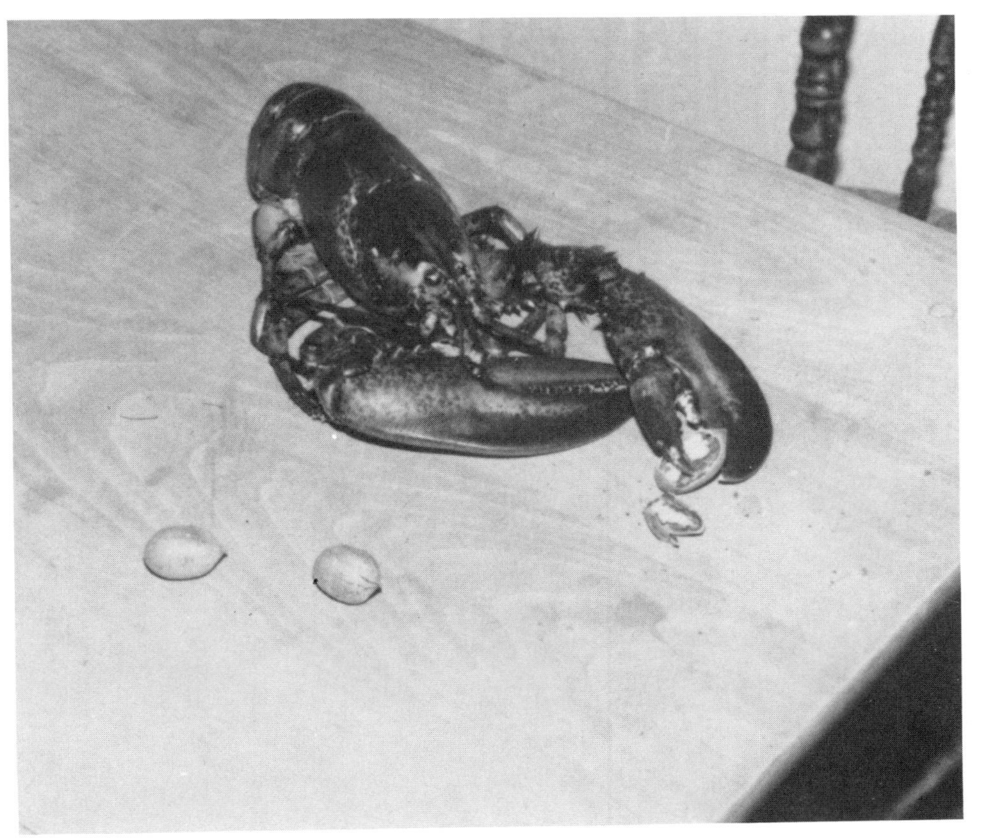

MAKING BREAKFAST

When he feels the urge, Stuart will make breakfast for the whole family. One of his favorite lobster recipes is french toast.

CARE
&
FEEDING

A HEALTHY DIET MAKES A HEALTHY PET

A lobster always likes to feel just like one of the family. . .***"Where's the beef?"*** Got to keep an eye on the cholesterol.

A TRIP TO THE VET IS A MUST!

Make sure he has had all his shots, and it's a good time to get him measured to be sure he's not a short!

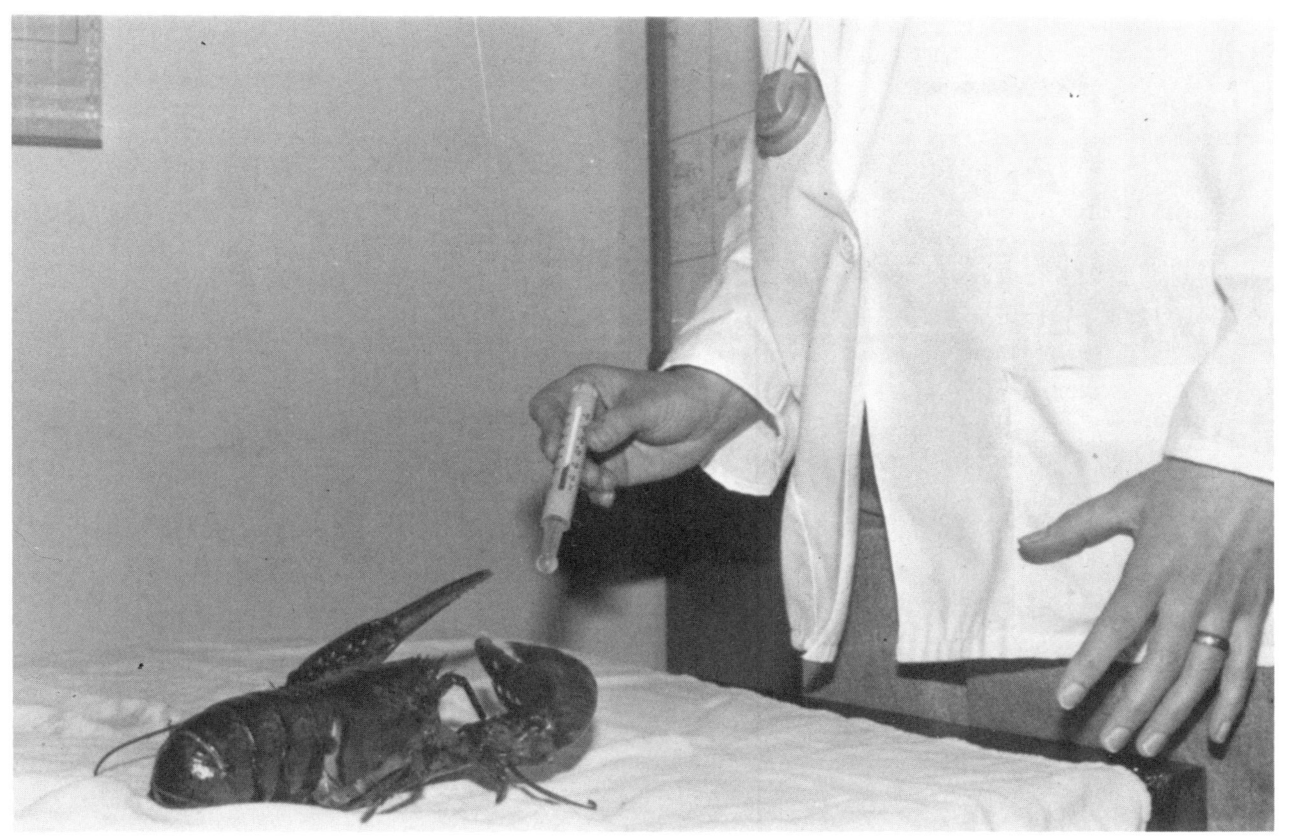

A DAILY WALK IS ALWAYS NEEDED

For a little exercise and a chance to check out the neighborhood, it's the best part of his day.

R117

VIGOROUS EXERCISE BUILDS MUSCLES!

Stuart makes a flying leap and snaps the disc in midair! ***Great catch, Pal. . .now, just bring it here!***

A BED OF HIS OWN

They will sleep about anywhere, but most lobsters prefer a nice, warm bed all by themselves.

MAKE SURE HE HAS A SAFE PLAYTHING

He may frolic for hours with a ball of yarn. . .***What's that you're knitting there, fella?***

LISTENING TO RELAX

Something about Rock and Roll must remind them of home. At high tide, Stuart likes to listen to the Rolling Stones. At low tide, he seems to prefer New Wave.

SHARP
STEREO

FUN & GAMES

SPEND QUALITY TIME TOGETHER

You'll be surprised at how quickly these little fellas learn! Now Stuart's trying to fill a straight. He needs to get out of a pinch!

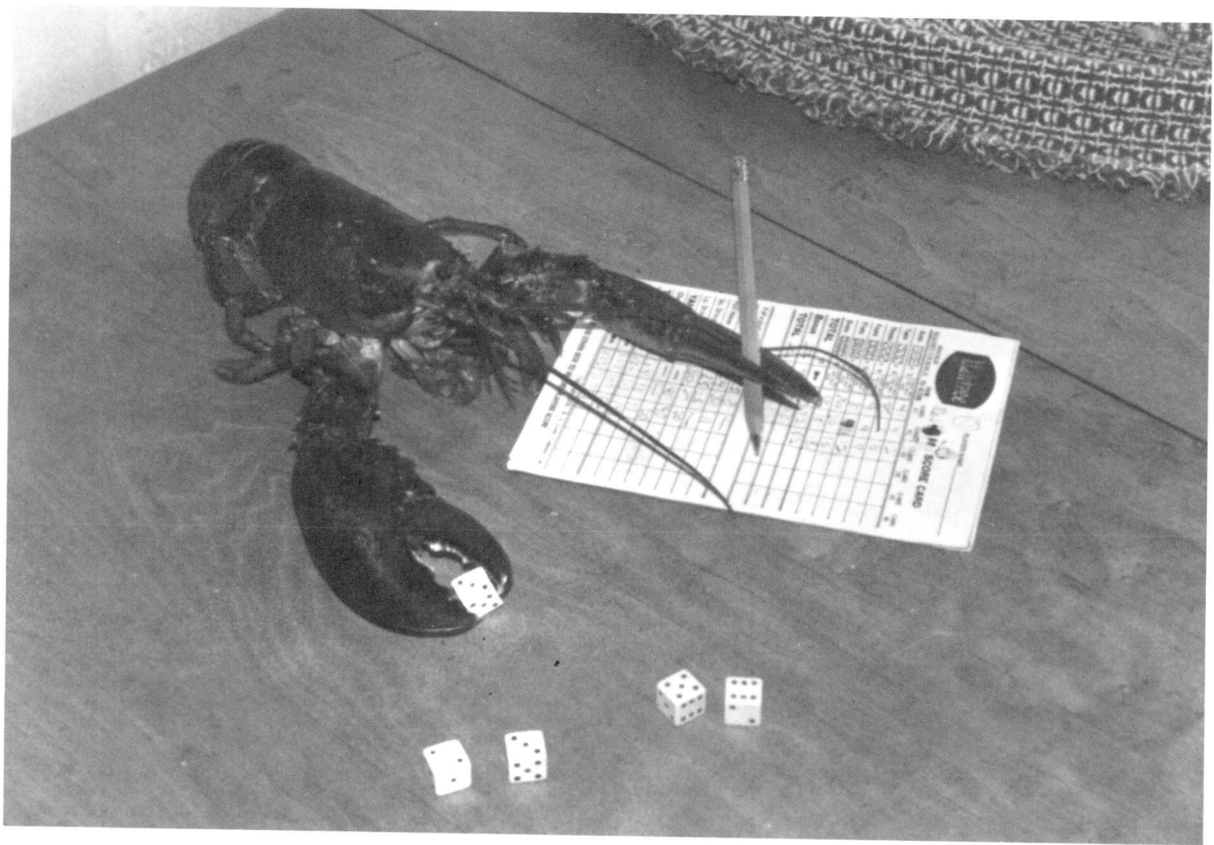
TOTAL
SCORE CARD

A GAME OF CRIBBAGE

It's uncanny how much lobsters enjoy a good game of cribbage. Maybe it's something about pegging that appeals to them.

A CLOSE GAME

In the end game, the same as in the refrigerator, Stuart knows the thing to watch out for is a stale mate!

A DAY AT THE PIER

Most lobsters love to go fishing. Be sure to set the drag light enough so the big one won't get away. . .with the lobster in tow!

FIND HIM A GOOD HOBBY

Everyone needs something to fill that extra time, and your new pet will be no exception. We got him a kit, and now Stuart is busy building a depth finder.

ON TOP OF OLD SMOKEY

Although it's quite unusual, Stuart seemed to pick up the harmonica in a snap. His favorite song is "Old Smokey" and his favorite note is high sea.

DOWN IN THE VALLEY

PAINTING WITH OILS

Stuart's style goes back to the style of the British portrait painters, as his admired artist is Samuel Found Bottom Moss.

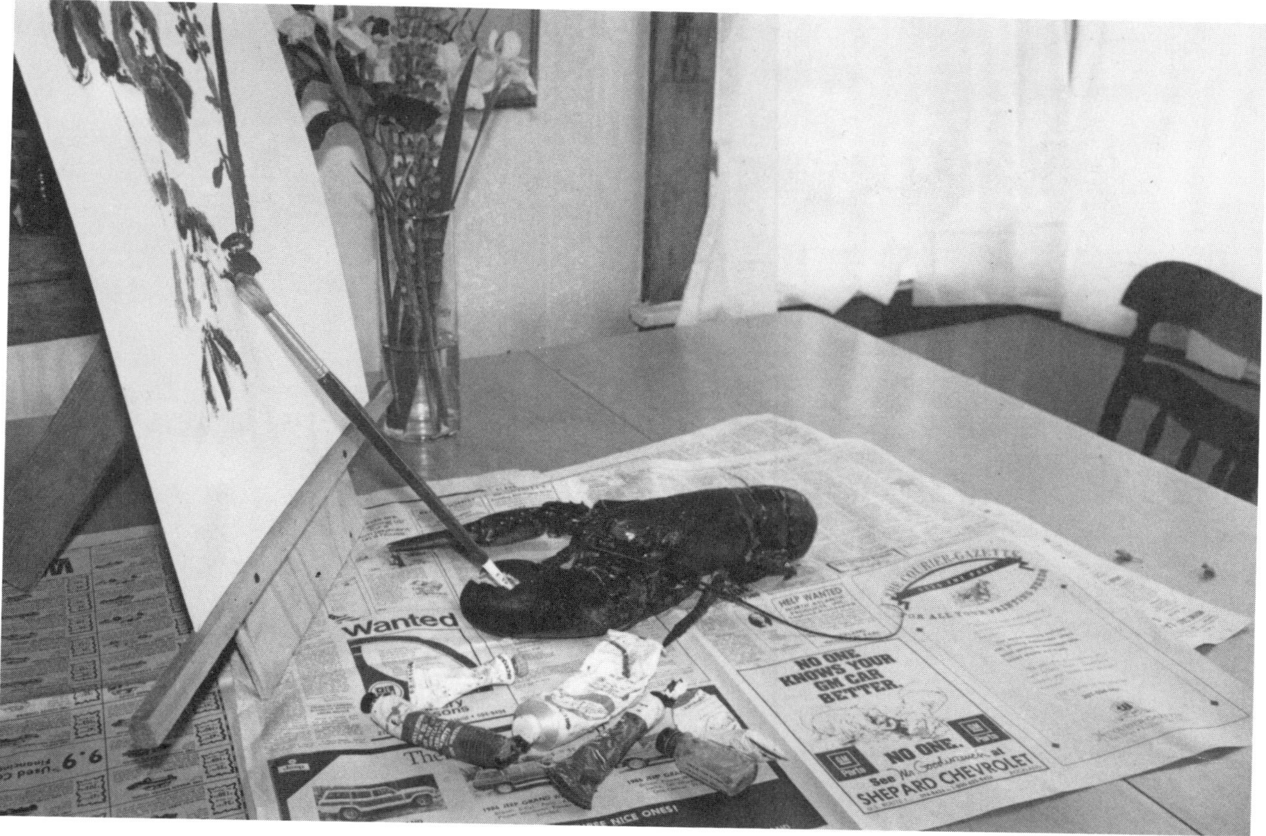
Wanted
HELP WANTED
NO ONE KNOWS YOUR GM CAR BETTER.
NO ONE.
SHEPARD CHEVROLET

TAKE HIM SKATING

Your lobster may be a bit timid about being the only crustacean on the floor, but once he gets used to it, you'll really see a lobster roll!

SLEIGHT-OF-CLAW

Stuart plays a version of the shell game, just for fun. See if you can find the periwinkle.

ARCADE KING

Your lobster can get really excited during the fierce action of video games. Stuart often crushes the competition, and sometimes the joystick!

THE SOCIAL LOBSTER

MAKING FRIENDS

Of course, your lobster will be shy at first, but having a friend to talk with—even on the phone—will help him to get out of his shell.

GIVE HIM CHORES

To develop a sense of self-worth and good work habits, give your pet a job to do around the house.

THE NEED FOR DISCIPLINE

You may feel like beating him with a newspaper if he gets into trouble, but you'll get better results by imposing restrictions. And be firm!

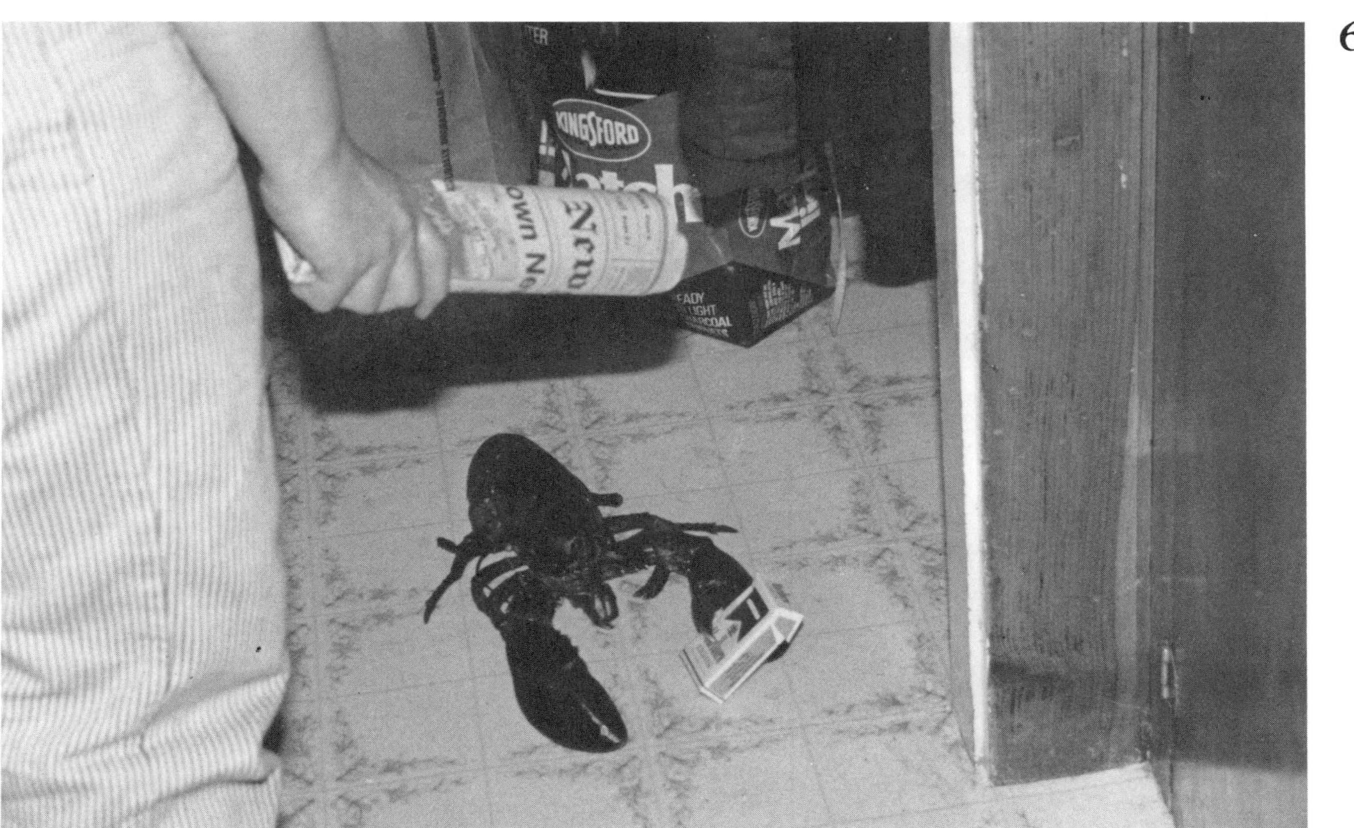
KINGSFORD

HAVING A FRIEND OVER

Lobsters love to party. You may want to keep an eye on things, though, so they don't get too wild and crazy.

THE CHANNEL SELECTOR

You may find out that a lobster's span of attention is really short. If he has the selector, he'll keep changing the station. Stuart keeps looking for "Sea Hunt."

TEACHING GOOD MONEY HABITS

Saving is something that doesn't come easily to most lobsters. But you can teach them to pinch pennies by praising them and matching funds with them if they stick with it.

SOME DOs & DON'Ts

A WORD OF CAUTION IN THE BATH!

Make sure you check the tub before crawling in, or you just might get a surprise!

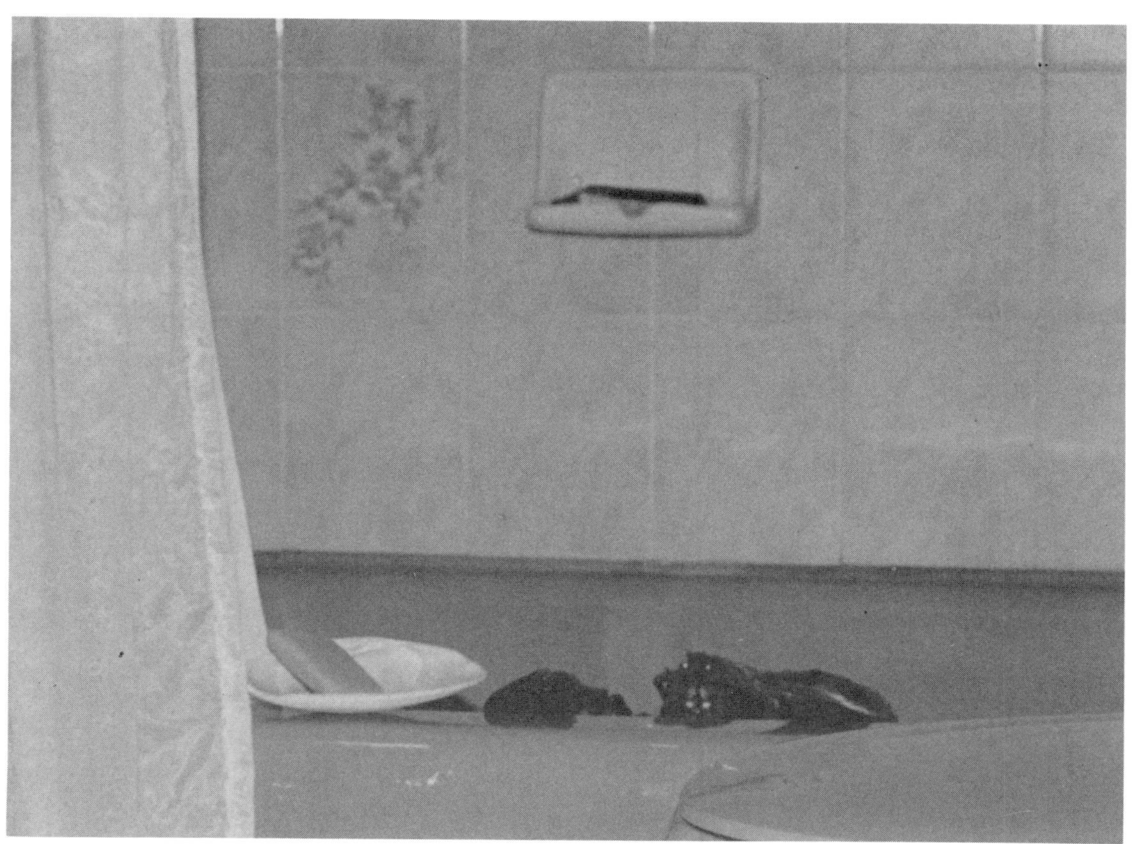

SAFETY FIRST AROUND TREES

If your lobster climbs up too high in a tree, he may need help getting down. Just speak in a calm voice, and don't forget that he may be somewhat disoriented.

SOME THINGS ARE BEST KEPT HIDDEN

Lobsters generally do not have a good understanding of credit. If they find your credit card lying around, you could receive some unexpected billings. Stuart ordered 100 Salad Wizards.

CHECKING YOUR LEASE

If you live in a rented apartment or a leased home, you may want to check your lease to see if it says anything about keeping a lobster on the premises. You may want to have a lawyer write you up a lobster clause.

ONE LAST WORD OF WARNING!

Something you should never, **never** do is to take your lobster in for a little swim! We sure do miss our old lobster, Stu!

Weston Arey, born in Camden, Maine, "some time ago," has always lived near the coast of Maine. "You've got to live somewhere; it might as well be to home, if you can stand it. Besides, if I moved, I'd have to clean out the attic."

He is a licensed contractor with a wife and three children, two still at home. His background, he insists, would not make good reading.

"But I will give you some advice. When you go to a restaurant, look out the window. If you can't see the ocean, order the steak."

Asked about his unusual pets, he replies, "Well, I never met a lobster I didn't like."